THE WORLD IS MY OFFICE

THE COMPLETE GUIDE TO BEING A DIGITAL NOMAD

Table Of Contents

1: The World is My Office

2: Starting Out

3: What to Expect

4: Common Mistakes

5: Golden Rules of Freelancing

6: How to Find Work

7: Problems to Prepare For

8: Important Things to Consider

9: Organisation

10: Money & Taxes

11: Preparing for Your Future

12: Your First Client

13: Revenue Streams

14: Don't Forget About Travel

15: Is This for You?

THE WORLD IS MY OFFICE

Just years ago you may have commuted to a conventional, traditional office environment and endured a nine to five job surrounded by colleagues, today, things can be much different. In the life of a digital nomad, the whole world becomes the 'office'. Digital technologies have opened a world (literally) of opportunities for those of us who wish to revolutionise the way in which we work and where we work.

With many choosing to work from the comfort of their own homes or rented office space, 'digital nomads' as the affectionate term dictates, use the technologies at their disposal to make an income from any location with an internet connection. Let's look at how others define the term 'digital nomad'. I'll do this in the hope that it gives you a more concrete insight into the lifestyle that one would lead when choosing not to work following the 'conventional nine to five office job' lifestyle.

This is all to prepare you for what comes next, where I'll be looking at what it means to be a digital nomad under the microscope; giving you an insight into the lifestyle and giving helpful tips that will inform you of what to expect. This will all be before analysing whether this lifestyle is really for you. BecomeNomad.com defines the digital nomad lifestyle as the following;

> *"Living the Digital Nomad Lifestyle means relying on the internet to financially sustain a modern nomadic life. This relatively new trend allows you to become location independent and constantly move between cities as countries while working remotely"*

BecomeNomad.com effectively describes the freedom you will find with the digital nomad lifestyle. Rather than being confined to just the one desk in a typical nine to five office job, the life of a digital nomad is more flexible, freeing and more importantly, it's far more exciting. BecomeNomad.com uses the term 'location independent', which effectively describes the very notion of what the lifestyle entails.

A digital nomad can work for people/organisations from various countries over the internet, or if the job requires, a nomad can take flights to constantly move between cities and countries, working remotely across the globe when the situation dictates it.

As the definition explains, this is still a relatively new 'trend', if that's the word you want to apply. Though, 'trend' kind of implies that its lifespan is limited and the excitement of it will soon wear off. I don't believe this is the case. Rather, this is a new way of 'the working life', where we are no longer confined to such a small working space, stuck in one office doing the same thing each day.

Digital technologies are more effective, efficient and are constantly evolving. Accessible communication methods are allowing us to see opportunities for work that we would have never known about twenty years ago. Freelance and remote workers are expected to rise excessively by the year 2020 and of course, at some point, this will curve and begin to drop but it is vital to seek this lifestyle whilst it is not saturated.

This shows just how much digital technologies have developed in such a short space of time. It is now at a point where we can not only revolutionise the conventional office workspace, but we can revolutionise our working lifestyle. Now, jobs are available at the click of a mouse and the refresh of a webpage.

Gone are the days of needing to take your CV around to multiple businesses in the hope that one may just read it. Gone are the days of being stuck in a dead-end job and are confined to one location. Gone are the days of working 'normally', if you're ready for it.

The popularity of this lifestyle isn't just being seen from the point of view of a digital nomad, but it is also more popular with modern-day companies. Companies that are able to visualise the benefits of working in a more agile way are reaping the benefits of those living a digital nomad lifestyle.

It's proving that many individuals and organisations alike are recognising the many flaws involved with working the way most of us did before, in a conventional environment confined to just one desk.

Companies are beginning to understand that hiring a digital nomad means you save on office space. Also, it is more cost-effective to hire somebody freelance rather than having permanent members of staff in place for 'when it gets busy'. This allows for more flexibility and means the company can find somebody who better suits a candidate's specification for that particular project, rather than trying to find a permanent member of staff who can do everything, as these people usually come at a hefty salary cost to an employer.

Many companies have already recognised these benefits and implemented this way of life into their business models, going fully remote with employees and/or freelancers around the world. Even some of the largest organisations hire remote workers including Apple, Google, and Amazon.

There are many misconceptions when it comes to the term 'digital nomad'. People often believe that it's not a 'real job' and that the people living this way are just lounging in the sun in some exotic country, carelessly and very slowly typing away at a laptop.

Many people do not appreciate just how much time, effort, patience, and willpower is needed to withstand a career like this. Though we would all like a job where we could lay down on a tropical beach and work when we felt the urge to, it's an unrealistic lifestyle and the people with the mindset haven't really thought it through. If there are people out there who are living up to this common misconception, the truth is, they won't be for much longer. It's just not feasible.

Though I have maybe shown the life of a digital nomad in a glamorous light, is not an easy one and isn't for the faint-hearted. It takes hard work, perseverance and a willingness to power through adversity.

Like all jobs and all ways of life, it isn't without its challenging and tough times though and it may involve taking risks, working with those you do not know very well or trust just yet and wondering at times where the next cheque is going to come from.

You must be adaptable; I like to think of a digital nomad as one of the earth's chameleons. A chameleon of the earth can work wherever he/she wants and is able to change or adapt themselves in order to match the situation they're in. Whether they're needing to work from a coffee shop during a spare hour in their day, foreign countries for important jobs or public libraries because it's the only place they can focus at that very point in time.

A digital nomad shouldn't have too many procedures or requirements in place that need to be met before working. They should instead meet the requirements of the job at hand.

With the world as your office, there's literally a world of opportunities out there. You just need to know how to find them, how to live a successful digital nomad lifestyle and more importantly, if the lifestyle is for you. That's where this guide comes in, as we'll be covering all of this and more as you read on.

I'll give you everything you need to know in order to send you on your way, well-equipped with the tools and knowledge you need in order to begin your journey as a digital nomad. Or, if it's not for you, at least you've explored the option and learned about all its benefits and drawbacks. I hope you find the guide informative, interesting and last but not least, useful.

Please remember, if you're still not entirely sold on which way to take your career after reading this guide, consider that there are still many other avenues for you to explore and you don't need to have a concrete answer today.

Think on it, explore your options and if need be, speak to a career advisor and maybe read a few of the personal development books in your local library or alternatively, online.

Without further ado, let's learn more about the life of a digital nomad and everything it entails.

STARTING OUT

Beginning your life as a digital nomad isn't quite as easy as just saying it. There's so much more to it than that, but when it's done right it can be the most rewarding, gratifying thing in the world.

Starting out your life as a digital nomad requires preparation, research, planning and more importantly, a willingness to learn. Without an open mind, you, unfortunately, won't have what it takes to survive as one and therefore may be a job in a conventional office environment is the right avenue for you. If, however, you are willing to learn, become adaptable and show you have what it takes, let's do this.

In this chapter, I'll give you all the information you need to know when beginning your digital nomad lifestyle. I think we should give it a title, like… 'reincarnation'. This is your 'digital nomad reincarnation'. Where before you were somebody who may have been confined to just one desk working in the conventional nine to five office setting, you are now reincarnated as a digital butterfly, growing wings, taking off and seeing that there is much more to the world than what you saw in your trapped life before. If you want to see it from an evolutionary point of view, you've finally shed your cocoon.

Now that you're beginning this new 'life', you can't just go out and take on the world with no tools or knowledge at your disposal. After all, your life before likely hasn't taught you much about the working world around you and that's where I come in. So, if you're ready, let's do this - let's give you the tools you need to become a fully-fledged digital nomad.

Ask Yourself 'The Question

Okay, you're probably now wondering what 'the question' is and there's an easy explanation. Before you can even go on to gain the knowledge and understanding of the digital nomad lifestyle and the tools you'll need for success, you must first look for answers from within. I don't mean spiritually or anything like that, but rather you should be asking yourself the necessary questions you need answers to before you can even proceed with this guide.

The first being the most important "Is the digital nomad lifestyle for me?". This is a question you should continue to ask yourself from this point on and every time you learn something new about the digital nomad lifestyle. This is for your own sanity and to ensure you're making the right choice.

I would strongly recommend asking yourself this each time you hear something new about this way of life, as this way you are allowing yourself to be critical of the process, whether you're on side from the get-go or you already have your concerns. This way, you make a better, more informed decision by the time you finish the guide and you've allowed each piece of information to register and be put under the microscope.

You may be surprised to hear that many people don't even consider this and are sold on the 'dream' of the digital nomad lifestyle, often ignoring or rather sidestepping the drawbacks of being one and purely focusing on the benefits, without seeing or wanting to see the wider picture.

The people who operate this way are often setting themselves up for failure, or at least a delay in significant success. This is largely because they haven't subjected themselves to some of the harsher realities of the lifestyle and therefore aren't equipped with the right tools to effectively combat them.

This is why it's so important to learn as much as you can about the lifestyle and judge it for yourself, your wants and needs and if you think you've got what it takes. Other people cannot make this decision for you and they definitely shouldn't influence your choice. It needs to be right for you, and if it's not, then it's simply not the career path for you.

Do Not Sell All of Your Possessions

This is a common misconception when people are beginning their new lives as digital nomads, just because there's the potential to travel the world when opportunities for work become available, it doesn't mean you should be free of materialistic possessions.

This may become a necessity to a certain degree later on in your career as a digital nomad, but it very much depends on the varying levels of success that can be achieved when living this kind of lifestyle. I would recommend that you continue as you are, taking on new jobs that suit your skillset, as and when they become available and only selling your possessions when it is absolutely necessary.

For instance, if you know you're going to be away from home for the next year, you may need to slim down what you own, but even in circumstances like this, other options are available depending on your finances at the time.

Storage unit solutions are an effective means of storing your essential items (if you're going to go rent-free in your home country). Storage solutions seem to be becoming cheaper by the day, so it's an option worth exploring and depending on the time you will be away for, many companies in this industry offer discounted rates for 6+ months signed off at once.

Alternatively, you likely have friends and family that can assist you when it comes to freeing up your life of your materialistic possessions, at least for the time in which you think you'll need to. As I said, you can always shed the excess (everything that isn't essential), but only if you believe you're genuinely at that level of productivity and busyness that warrants it. If the storage option isn't for you, speak to friends and family and request help storing your essentials from them.

Reduce Ties and Expenses

Tying into the first point I made, though you shouldn't blitz your life of everything you own and cancel contracts or everything and your rent, you should rather consider where you could save money and free yourself up for the digital nomad world you're about to enter.

There may be several things currently tying you to one location, and it can be difficult to let those things go, particularly if you're not even sure it's the right time to let go of them. It's always best, like I said, to evaluate everything.

The most common things that tie people to one country, and often a specific location within that country, are contracts on cars and houses. If you're in a long-term contract then it can be very difficult to get out of it before the end date, but don't let this deter you from your aspirations.

If you're serious enough and you're confident that you'll find work, then you need to be able to travel light and more importantly, travel without much expense. Do your best to work through these contractual obligations but always ensure your financial stability before setting out on your digital nomad journey.

After recognising the two biggest ties for the majority of people, you can then look at the smaller, less-important expenses like gym memberships and streaming services. The key is, if you can live without it then it should be a strong contender for cancellation.

> *At the end of the day, do you really need a gym membership for your hometown if you're travelling from location to location for different jobs?*

If the answer wasn't already clear enough, you should be logging into online banking and cancelling that Pure Gym direct debit right now.

Debts are another important thing to consider before you head out to start your digital nomad journey. Though it's likely you're in little to no debt at all, for those of you who are, you need to settle them in some shape or form before you start out on your new career pathway.

The most effective way of dealing with them while you're away is to first set up payment plans. These payment plans provide structure to your debt, allowing you to pay what you genuinely believe you can pay, making your finances clearer while you're away and ensuring that debt doesn't continue to mount up.

One-Way Tickets Should Be Avoided

As I said earlier in this guide, it's easy to fall for the life of a digital nomad when reading about it on paper, exploring the world, working on different projects and having the ability to face a new challenge every day. Unfortunately, it isn't as glamorous as some people would have you believe, and you shouldn't be sold on a dream. It requires a lot of hard work and planning, and you definitely should think twice before diving in with both feet.

Like any professional dive, it requires choreography, careful planning and consideration, and rehearsals. The rehearsals should be you thinking over and over about what your best move is. I would recommend you have confidence without allowing that confidence to slip into delusion, as that can be dangerous.

Just because you're going to work on one project in another country, doesn't mean that's now going to be your life. One-way plane tickets should be avoided unless you have the paperwork to say 'this is what I'm going to be doing for the foreseeable future' or you're confident (not delusional) that it's going to work out. Without that, you're taking a huge leap of faith that you may not be ready for.

Identify Your Skills

Please consider that this list is in no particular order and no one thing is more important than the other. The list is simply a guide on the avenues you should explore when starting out your new lifestyle of a digital nomad. Your 'reincarnation' process requires you to consider all the points brought forward in this chapter, so you can effectively understand the lifestyle, see if it's for you and give you the information you need to get going. That said, it's time to identify your skills if you haven't already.

A crucial building block in the foundation of preparing for your digital nomad lifestyle, identifying your skillset. This is absolutely necessary if you're going to stand any chance at success. If you can't tell somebody the skills you've acquired and where your strengths lie, you're unfortunately going to struggle.

A key to surviving as a digital nomad is to know yourself inside and out, being able to talk yourself up and show people what you're good at. Whether you're an ambitious and creative designer or you're the numbers guy, people need to know it, and the only way they'll ever know it is if you do too, and you can shout about it.

A key point to consider would be to note down your most valuable skills and take a look at the available remote jobs that are out there. If you find that you can only relate to 2% off them, it is likely that you would struggle to find work/projects. Identifying a weakness in your skillset will enable you to seek out training and courses to develop the skills you would need to cover remote jobs.

Learn to Be Adaptable

I know, I keep saying it, but if you aren't already then you need to learn how to be adaptable if you can find it in yourself to have the capacity for change. With being a digital nomad comes many challenges you have likely never faced before, but the person who hired you for the project your working on doesn't want to hear those problems and challenges, he/she wants to see results. The time may come when you're working in remote areas without good infrastructure, without the facilities we often take for granted in further developed countries.

This is where you need to be able to think on your feet, effectively plan and adapt to the situation you find yourself. After all, you cannot just go back to the company who hired you and say "I didn't finish the marketing campaign because I couldn't find any Wi-Fi. It simply won't suffice. As I said, they want to see results, so if you don't have access to the internet, find it... and quick.

You need to get creative when it comes to where and how you will work. Particularly if you're struggling to find options for internet access, you may end up having to track down a cafe in the middle of nowhere just to use their Wi-Fi. It's key to remember that when living the life of a digital nomad, your 'office' is ever-changing, and you need to be able to adapt to the situation you're forced into.

Yes, that can sometimes include powering through your work even though everybody in the cafe is so loud that it's difficult to think. I have been in numerous situations where I had no access to Wi-Fi, my laptop charger broke, power cuts and even having to work from my iPhone.

Try It

The only way to really know you're going to like the life of a digital nomad isn't to learn about it in theory but is to put it into practice and try the lifestyle out for yourself before you make any kind of important decision.

It may be worth checking with your current employer to see if they would allow you to begin working from home for a period of time. More and more companies today are open to the idea of more agile working practices, even if it is taking a long time for particular industries to get up to speed.

Most employers too should be encouraging your personal development, so hopefully, they will be open to the idea if you're willing to make a strong enough case for it. Where that isn't possible (certain employers, particularly in more traditional fields likely won't allow you to work from home), take on freelance jobs in your own time to get a flavour for working in a different setting, adapting to the working life outside of a well-equipped, conventional office environment.

Though it may seem like a lot of planning and preparation to get 'digital nomad ready' it's far better to do this while you're still in full-time work than find out the hard way later down the line when you've freed yourself of your contractual obligations and tried it for real all by yourself. The more planning you do and the more practice you get in, the clearer this way of life will be in your mind.

Learn How to Manage Your Finances

I know, it's easier said than done. This one kind of ties into what I was saying in the first two points regarding freeing yourself of unnecessary expenditures and sorting out 'your house' before beginning your digital nomad journey. This point is rather concerning itself with thinking about the notion of saving up money and evaluating your potential purchases before you make them.

Think of your journey into the career pathway of a digital nomad in the same way you would think about going on a trip, because that's essentially what you are doing anyway, just this time it's for work.

No matter what trip you're going on, digital nomad or not, it's always a good idea to save up money in preparation. You never know what might happen when you get out there and you never know just how much money you might need.

It's always good to try and work out how much you might need, being as realistic as you possibly can of course. That way, you can use this number as a guide for how much you will actually take. I'd always recommend taking slightly more than you'd expect to spend; it's better to be safe than sorry is all I'm thinking.

Both before and during your trip as a digital nomad butterfly (see what I did there?), managing your finances effectively is crucial. Unfortunately, this means evaluating your purchasing habits, ensuring, at least until your properly on your feet and doing well for yourself that you're spending your money on the right things. When you're just starting out, it's always better to just ask yourself one simple question, "Do I need it?".

It's a piece of advice we should all really follow, no matter what walk of life we're from, we'd certainly all save a good bit of money by following that piece of advice anyway. I know it's easier said than done, but that's the case for everybody looking to take advice on their finances, at the end of the day, nothing is ever easy.

By asking yourself the question "Do I need it?" each time you feel tempted to make a purchase, you'll find yourself refining your purchasing processes, only buying what is necessary to function and maintain your newfound digital nomad lifestyle.

Rather than renting a house full of display pieces you wanted but never really needed, you're free to work anywhere in the world, only buying what you humanly need to survive and thrive.

That's the key, make purchases to survive and thrive... or your career as a digital nomad just might die. This is purely just advice to follow, and it won't be as relevant for those of you with deeper pockets to start with. I'm simply going by what the average person's pockets will be like. It is by no means an accurate representation of the financial situation of every reader.

> *"...make purchases to survive and thrive, or your career as a digital nomad just might die".*

With the information I've provided you in this chapter, I hope you can recognise just how much preparation needs to be involved when you're making the transition from a conventional office job to the revolutionary life of a digital nomad.

That said, the preparation is worth it and more, or at least it can be if you're willing to consistently and continually put the work in. The life of a digital nomad is an exclusive group, and though access to it is easy, maintaining your access to it is not without its challenges.

By following all the key points within this chapter, you're well on your way to leading a successful digital nomad lifestyle, full of prosperity, personal-growth and hopefully fantastic opportunities that allow you to travel the world.

In the following chapter, we'll take a look at what you should expect from your upcoming digital nomad lifestyle in the hopes of further preparing you for what's to come. As with all the information I present to you in this guide, none of it is intended to discourage you from pursuing the lifestyle, but rather to give you a real insight into what it's going to be like for you when/if you decide to take the plunge and take a leap of faith.

Many other sources on the internet will sell you a fantastical version of what the reality is really like for a digital nomad, unfortunately persuading people into a career path that they might not be ready for at that point in time. This is something I want to avoid at all costs as I believe in being transparent with you. At the end of the day, it is no benefit of mine to push you to a career change that may not be for you.

My main interest is to inform you of a new means of working in today's world, where digital technologies can provide us with the capabilities of working remotely, from location to location around the world.

By the end of the guide, I want you to believe you're making an informed, educated decision based on what you genuinely believe to be the best move for you, considering all the points made in this guide, particularly this chapter. Make the best move for you, and don't be sold on dreams.

WHAT TO EXPECT

On paper, the life of a digital nomad appears to be the dream many people on the internet would have you believe. However, if you're taking into account what you're seeing from your digital nomad peers on social media, I have one important piece of advice that I pray you'll respond to. Don't.

Social media, though powerful, inspiring and thought-provoking, doesn't always provide an accurate representation of reality. On social media, people are able to show you an altered (filtered, of course) version of their reality as a means of bragging rights.

Though it seems a shame to say this and of course, not everybody actively using social media behaves in this way, many people unfortunately do and therefore it's important not to fall into the trap. At the end of the day, you should believe what you see and experience it with your own eyes when it happens in a natural setting.

It's key to remember that when you see a post on social media, often much preparation has gone into that post; people (likely including yourself) will self-edit, portraying their lives in a very specific way in order to give you a detailed, carefully crafted (if not unrealistic) snapshot insight into their lifestyle.

Chances are, if you're seeing a digital nomad posting that he/she is on the beach with a cocktail whilst working, they probably posted that later on that same day in a dark and dingy internet cafe that they had to walk two hours to find, besides who can see their laptop screen in the sun?

In this chapter, I would like to show you what you should really expect, rather than relying on the Instagram accounts of your peers to provide you with knowledge of the lifestyle of a digital nomad. As I've said throughout this guide, I would like to provide you with a real insight, as I'm not a salesman; I'm not trying to sell you onto my conference of 'how to be a successful digital nomad'.

There is no such course available from me, and I'm all about providing you with the information you need to make an informed decision. There's no sales pitch here.

"So, what should I expect?" you may be wondering by this point in the chapter and it's a good question, let's take a look.

Rejection

Life as a digital nomad isn't plain sailing from start to finish, especially when you're just starting out. Be prepared for rejection, and lots of it. "Your rate is too expensive", or "Your projected delivery date is too late for us", no matter the reason, rejection is present in the life of a digital nomad and that's why this career path isn't for the faint-hearted. Rather than letting the rejections get you down, you need to persevere and use what you've been told to work on the services and skills you offer.

If you weren't given a reason for your rejection, then you have two options; you can ask the company you were looking to work with for some feedback or alternatively, you can instead work on a self-evaluation. Self-evaluation is key when leading a digital nomad life as you can't rely on a manager/supervisor/owner for regular feedback on your performance or work ethic.

By practicing regular self-evaluation, you should be able to recognise your strengths, flaws, and areas for improvement, allowing you to take the necessary steps to ensure you do a better job next time, or in this case, get the job that you missed out on.

If you were given the feedback that your delivery date was too late, then you need to look at how you can offer shorter delivery dates. You need to ask yourself what needs to be done in order to turn work around faster and guarantee the client is happy, ensuring you get the job and are considered for future jobs.

If it means missing out on an hour of recreational time each day just to get the work turned around faster, I would recommend you lose the hour of recreational time and use your time proactively.

Varying Rates of Success

This point is crucial, particularly if you've fallen for the dream of becoming a digital nomad. You may be expecting to enter the (entire) world of work and be met with open arms and nice juicy cheques. This, however, isn't always the case, particularly if you've not put your name out there before, or if you have had any negative experiences with larger, more influential clients in the past.

Expect varying rates of success, as the subheading states. When you're first starting out, it may take some time for the work to come through. This is largely because you don't have the same track record of many of the people living the same kind of lifestyle you have chosen to follow. Now, the other digital nomads are almost like your competitors, or at least the ones offering the same services you are anyway.

Many established digital nomad professionals will have work coming through thick and fast, often receiving recommendations as they move from company to company, from location to location. This, however, is not the reality when you're still fresh-faced to the lifestyle.

You need to build up to where your peers in the same field may be, undercutting their rates, delivery times and going above and beyond to get that business over your more successful 'competitors'.

It's always a slow-moving process, so of course, it requires patience, but when it means you can travel the world and work for many companies and grow as a person, it makes it all worth it. It's certainly more exciting than a conventional nine to five job if you're prepared to put the hard work in.

A Lack of Income, at First

Tying into the point above, regarding the varying rates of success, it's highly likely that when you're first starting out as a digital nomad, you may experience life with a lack of income. In the previous chapter, we talked about how saving money and effectively managing your finances was crucial, well this is why.

By saving money in preparation for beginning your life as a digital nomad, you will be able to dip into those savings if your financial situation isn't as healthy as you'd like it to be, at least until those new jobs come in and the income streams begin flowing.

If you're somebody who likes structure and stability, this will certainly be a difficult change for you, but it doesn't necessarily mean that the life of a digital nomad isn't for you. Rather, it instead takes some getting used to and requires you to put the extra work in to ensure you can get the money coming in and sustain the lifestyle.

Chances are, when you first get going, your income is going to be significantly less than your peers but keep at it and with some luck, you'll be good.

Side Hustles

Okay, maybe the term hustle shouldn't be used when I'm speaking in a business context, but I'm using the term playfully in order to make my point. Linking to the two points above, when your income streams are few and far between and/or lower than you expected them to be, you may be required to work a few 'side-hustles' in order to pay the bills.

"What might these side-hustles be?"

Well, I had a friend in Australia who found herself in this position and rather than accept the doom and gloom of financial instability, she dusted herself off and went out and took anything she could find to make ends meet. She ended up taking a couple of shifts in a local internet cafe, she did a few cleaning shifts at a local hotel and even worked a few promotional events and shifts at pop-up/event shops.

Though these kinds of jobs weren't the reason she travelled to Australia in the first place, she found herself between two significant jobs and found things to keep her occupied in the meantime. These jobs allowed her to pay the bills and more importantly, eat. She recognised the situation she had found herself in and crafted a solution, pro-actively analysing the situation and looking for ways to resolve it. This is exactly the mindset a digital nomad should have in order to survive this way of life.

Though this may not be the ideal approach for some of you as you are journeying into your life of being a digital nomad, in the early days you, unfortunately, have to do what it takes to make ends meet. Grit and bear it until you've got your name out there enough and the workflow is more consistent, then you won't need side hustles at all or at least that's the dream for most budding digital nomads.

No Work at All

An even more frightening prospect for a budding digital nomad than working a job he/she doesn't want to do - having no work at all or losing a job very suddenly. These two possibilities seem drastic but are unfortunately very frequent occurrences in the world of working remotely/freelancing.

Without the stability of the conventional nine to five job where there's a guaranteed salary at the end of each month, working life for a digital nomad can be much different. The term most people who have implemented this way of life refer to it as 'unpredictable'. A bitter-sweet term that can be both positive and negative, but often, unfortunately, is used when you're dealt a bad hand.

The unpredictability of this way of working, unfortunately, means that if you're working for a company on a project and something within that project goes wrong or there's a funding issue, the freelancer/digital nomad is often the first person to go.

It's just the way it goes, as companies will almost always do what they can to protect their fixed assets and unfortunately see the non-permanent members of the team as disposable, regardless of how effective their input has been up to that point.

With the unpredictability of the digital nomad life, I would always recommend that you have one or two side hustles to fall back on. Though nobody wants to do a side-hustle when they can be flexing their main skill set, there's no shame in taking a job to simply pay for your necessities.

These side hustles also help you to grow as a person and teach you about a wide variety of different fields within business, allowing you to broaden your horizons even when you're not working to your full potential in the job you originally intended to do. Your side hustle doesn't have to be physical work, it could be something as simple as working on a small project online with minimum pay, such as flipping Instagram accounts.

Loneliness

This is by far one of the most important aspects of what to expect when going out on your own and becoming a digital nomad. Loneliness itself can create a whole raft of thoughts, emotions, and responses, and that's never an ideal mix when you're about to work with professionals from around the world.

It's highly likely that when you arrive in a new area, you'll be confined to your new accommodation and unfortunately, loneliness and nobody to talk to is a horrible combination, as it only adds to the problem. Not knowing anybody in the new area you've found yourself living in can be very challenging, and it's something we've all likely experienced to varying degrees in our lives already.

Usually, however, we can always call on support from a friend or family member who can come visit us. This time, you're in a whole different country, so that's going to be tricky.

Luckily, there are ways to combat how you may feel when you're faced with this situation; that's right, you don't need to work alone. There are many options available to you and I'm going to share just a few of them with you.

Whilst you're busy working, you can also socialise too, you just need to know where to do it. Co-working spaces like certain hubs and internet cafes mean that you can work and talk to like-minded people at the same time. When you're feeling lonely, you won't believe just how powerful one conversation can be, it can really brighten up your day.

Alternatively, you can strike up conversations with staff members in the internet cafe you choose to visit, the same goes anywhere you decide to do your work. Though the staff members of the venue are trying to do their own jobs too (be mindful of that), it doesn't hurt to be friendly and ask about their day.

Digital nomad hubs and/or groups exist around the world too, so these are also a good opportunity to meet like-minded individuals who share your passion for globetrotting and revolutionising the way we work. These people are just like you, so get to know them and take an interest in what they're doing. The benefits of networking with fellow digital nomads can be fantastic, after all, they may recommend you to a company for something they can't do themselves. Always be positive, friendly and show a willingness to listen, especially as they're probably lonely too.

Too Much Work

At some point down the road when you have established yourself and built up a reputation, you should be prepared for an increase in workload. This is where it is vital you know what your workload limit is.

A common mistake digital nomads make is that they don't know when to say no. It's fantastic being offered more work and money, especially when you had barely any at the beginning, but taking on too much work can lead to stress, depression and even affect your productivity/quality of work.

I can't really give an insight into what "too much work" will be as that is something only you will know. I have previously balanced 2 full-time jobs, 4 "side hustles" a personal blog, full-time university, all whilst travelling the world. I can tell you that it becomes very difficult to stay on top and produce high-quality work.

The best thing to do in this situation is work out how long various pieces of work will take you and make a schedule so you know what you could potentially fit into your day. For example, you may find that it takes you 20 minutes to type 500 words, allow 30 minutes and block that out of your schedule at some point in the day.

COMMON MISTAKES

Sometimes, living the life of a digital nomad comes with a fair number of struggles and unnecessary problems. When starting out your new life as a digital nomad, you're likely to feel the urge to do something on the list I'm about to go through in this chapter. My honest advice is, don't, as there's a reason it's made it to the list of 'common mistakes'.

Many digital nomads have suffered the consequences of falling victim to at least one of the several mistakes on this list, so I'm going to make it my mission to ensure none of you reading this guide ever do the same. If you do, I did try to warn you (don't ask for a refund on the guide, that's all I'm saying).

As you're going through the list, it may be worthwhile to consider if any of your digital nomad peers (if you have any digital nomad peers) have fallen into any of these traps. If they have, you should already be able to recognise what went wrong and know not to do it.

Purchasing Top of the Range Equipment

This is without a doubt one of the most common mistakes across the world with companies and digital nomads/freelancers alike. We all like to have expensive branded products, but I'm here to tell you that you don't need it. YOU are the expensive product, the company is buying into you, not what brand laptop you have.

Though you need to be well-equipped for your task at hand, there's no reason you should have the latest Apple MacBook or $4,000 laptop, when you could have a just as efficient HP laptop for $300 with a very similar (if not better) specification for a much lower price.

I get it though, I really do. You want to make the best impression possible. You want to look the part, but that's not the most important thing. You need to show your worth in the quality of your work before you show your worth in expensive materialistic equipment (that let's face it, you probably don't need). Let your work speak for itself with the equipment you already have, or at the very most, equipment you can comfortably afford before you even consider lavish purchases.

The latest MacBooks, iPhones, and iPads are among the three biggest contenders for a digital nomad to overcome if he/she really stands a chance at success. You need to resist the temptation of the awfully expensive Apple products in favour of reasonably priced goods that can efficiently perform the tasks you need them to.

Don't break your back to pay for the top of the range goods when in reality, you're essentially paying a premium price for an apple on the back of your technology. Check the specification of the product you want from Apple and find something similar, if not better from one of their much cheaper competitors. You'll thank me later.

The money you save from buying a cheaper, just as efficient laptop (etc.), can instead be put aside for emergencies and travel. When you're living your life as a digital nomad, you never know when you're going to need to dip into that money, so it's more important than ever before that you've put some money aside.

It's important to remember that the only person concerning themselves with the brand of laptop you own, is you. I'm generalising here, so if you're like me and you don't care about the brand of your laptop as long as the specification does what you need it to, that's great - you're already well on your way to a successful start as a digital nomad.

For those of you who still have concerns regarding the brand, just know that most companies will not judge you based on the brands you own and use, they're going to judge you on the quality of your work. Also, just as good, if not better-quality documents can equally be produced on an HP laptop as they can on a MacBook. So, remember it this way - fruit is good you for, but Apple is not.

> *"...fruit is good for you, but Apple is not".*

Being Disorganised

Organisational skills are crucial when it comes to life as a digital nomad. Gone are the days of the structure you'd find in a conventional nine to five job. There are no more days where a manager is pressing you to meet deadlines and reminding you to complete tasks.

You've gone your own way and you're the manager of your own career, despite working for many different clients across the world (potentially). Organisational skills ensure you are punctual when it comes to meeting deadlines and ensures people take you seriously in the job you're being hired to do.

By meeting these deadlines due to your organisational skills, you'll ensure that people see you as the reliable, trustworthy worker you are. Though for many starting out as digital nomads, the reality is much different and it's such an easy mistake to make.

Maybe you're used to working for a company where it's almost impossible to miss deadlines as you constantly have somebody breathing down your neck. Now, those aspects of your working life are taken away and you need to learn to self-manage.

Luckily, going it alone doesn't mean you have to be all things to all people, including yourself. You can rely on many different applications on your smartphone and/or laptop/tablet in order to assist you with your organisational skills and scheduling.

There are many different applications you can use, but I would recommend Google Tracker, allowing you to effectively, efficiently self-manage and plan for your upcoming meetings and deadlines. You won't believe how handy it is, and how much you probably forget when there's nobody/nothing to prompt you. You won't be able to comprehend how you were ever able to function without it.

It's up to you how you manage your workload, some people find that writing a list every day makes them more focused and productive whilst others use every project management app available just to stay organised. I am an organised person, and I thought that I could manage everything in my head. I soon learned that this wasn't the case and I needed to implement some sort of organisation strategy to my day.

Not Taking a Break

Now, this may sound a bit foolish, as surely this means you're being as productive as humanly possible. In fact, this couldn't be further from the truth. Some scientists believe that our brains can only effectively function in twenty-minute intervals before needing a break.

Though many scientists disagree with this and believe it to be a longer period of time, the point still stands that either way, we all need to take regular breaks. Not only for our own sanity but to ensure our work is as strong as it can possibly be.

We would all like to be as efficient as possible, especially when deadlines are looming over us and it appears as though we might be running out of time, trust me, I've been there myself. But the best way to combat it is to not let the pressure get to you. Take regular breaks to refuel and recharge your batteries to ensure the work you are producing; is the quality your client is expecting.

Taking breaks also aids your analytical skills, since you're able to come back to your work with a fresh pair of eyes, look over the work you were doing previously and take a fresh approach. This fresh approach gives you a greater chance of picking up on any mistakes that may have been present in your work before and often allows you time to craft even stronger ideas on how to further improve your work.

Sometimes, taking a break is the most productive thing you can do. That is if you're seriously committed to the project. You need to be on the ball, and sometimes taking fifteen minutes out is the best idea to achieve the best outcome for you and the work and your client.

I would highly recommend that you go outside for a break every day. When you work from home it can be so easy to "forget" to go outside and take in some natural light with some fresh air. Staring at a screen all day is bad for your eyes, posture and even sanity. Take a lunch break and walk to the local park to get away from your computer for a period of time.

> *"Sometimes, taking a break is the most productive thing you can do".*

Travelling too fast

When it comes to travelling some people enjoy relaxing in sunny locations for 6-month periods and others prefer to move to a new city every 3-days. If you are the individual that prefers the latter, then I recommend that you rethink your travelling plans.

Being a digital nomad is hard enough when you are trying to juggle multiple projects and set up in a new location. When you move to a new location, you will frequently you will have to consider Wi-Fi, new sim cards, meeting new people, new time zones and most importantly money.

Travelling in short spaces of time can seriously leave a dent in your bank balance, trust me. Not only will you be forking out for new flight tickets and hotels in a short space of time, but you will also have to find the time to fit in all the sightseeing you want to do.

If you are a seasoned traveller then you would know that sightseeing does not come cheap, especially if you are country-hopping every week. If you really can't resist travelling so rapidly then the best thing you can do in this instance would be to research what you want to see and set aside a budget so you can at least monitor your cash flow.

Not Exercising

I can almost guarantee that not one of you reading would have thought about this one. When you work in a physical location you are more inclined to walk around the office or perhaps you have a physical job that encourages exercise throughout the day.

With remote work, you will find that you stay seated for extended periods of time or even stay in bed for excessive time periods. This is not good for your body and you will see rapid increases in weight and other health issues.

You should get up and walk around or stay active by hitting the gym or going for a run 2-3 times per week. You could even do something as simple as walking to a coffee shop to get your work done for the day. Any amount of exercise would be beneficial to you when you work from home.

Not Learning Continuously or At All

One thing I will mention is that you will not stay ahead of the competition (competition being other digital nomads/freelancers) if you do not learn new skills and update existing ones. This is relatable to every aspect of life but even more so in the digital world. Technology advances rapidly every single day and there are always new methods, terms, algorithms, and programs. The only way that you will be able to keep your projects/contracts/clients is to continuously stay up to date on the latest trends and changes.

A prime example that can be given here is Search Engine Optimization, which is now the fundamental factor when it comes to marketing. There are continuous updates and changes to how SEO works and for those that work in marketing, if you do not stay up to date with these changes you will not be effective on your projects and you will likely not land a job.

I would recommend that you take online courses to maximise your efficiency in the field you are in. Following that you should subscribe to news channels and various blogs to receive the latest updates on those subjects, that way you can always ensure you will perform your best and stay ahead of the competition.

The internet is full of online courses and there are many that you can take for free which can occasionally come with accreditations. Take every course you can that is relatable and try to obtain accreditations in your field. Putting this information on your CV and employee profiles will boost your success rate and stand out to employers.

It's important to note that you shouldn't do this just to bolster your CV, it should be done from a knowledge perspective in order for you to gain more understanding on a subject. If you rushed through a course and didn't take anything in, you would become stuck when the time comes to put that knowledge to the test.

GOLDEN RULES OF FREELANCING

Without a manager to tell you what to do, you're going to need to self-manage, but how can you be expected to do that without any form of training. Luckily, there are guidelines or rules that you can follow in order to give yourself the best chance of success. When it comes to freelancing, you likely need all the guidance you can get from people already living the digital nomad lifestyle and especially for you, a list of golden rules has been devised in order to help you power through your life away from the conventional working life.

It's important to highlight that you should not deviate from these golden rules, after all, the word 'golden' is right in there - this chapter is your treasure chest. Those who do not live their digital nomad lifestyle by following these key principles are often destined for failure.

Be Responsive

When you're entering the life of a digital nomad, you need to be on the ball with your communication. You need to be efficient with your admin and luckily, admin and communication go hand in hand. The best way of putting this into practice is setting yourself goals in order to ensure you keep in regular contact with your current clients and keep up with requests and enquiries from new clients.

It is crucial to therefore regularly maintain the platforms in which you advertise your services on; consistently checking for messages and being responsive to those that you have. As a mini golden rule within the golden rule of being responsive, you should aim to reply to all messages within one hour.

Keep in mind, due to the time differences, you may receive messages throughout the night, which will make it near impossible to reply within an hour, 100% of the time. The point stands, you need to motivate yourself and see things from the client's point of view.

Imagine you were a client that was in need of the services you're offering. If you sent somebody a message and didn't receive a reply all day, you would probably take this negatively. You'd probably be disappointed that in the freelancer's entire day, they didn't even have one minute to acknowledge your request - you're trying to pay them at the end of the day, so you'd think they would be motivated enough to reply.

If you're not entirely rushed off your feet all day every day, you should try and check in with current clients and inform them of the progress you're making with their projects. It's a nice little reminder to your current clients that you haven't forgotten about them and it highlights that you're passionate about your job.

You can go one step further too by checking in with old clients to see what happened with the projects you worked on in the past. This is also a great opportunity to remind old clients that you're still active and therefore putting you back on their radar.

Be responsive, stay respectful, and do your best to always say 'yes'. That's your best chance to not only survive but thrive. Always keep your unread message count at '0', after all, these potential clients are trying to spend money on your services, and you need money. You won't benefit in any way from ignoring potential opportunities.

> "Be responsive, stay respectful and do your best to always say 'yes'. That's your best chance to not only survive but thrive".

Motivation

With self-managing comes self-motivation. Motivation is a

golden rule of achieving success as a freelancer, as you're no longer motivated to do your work to avoid receiving flak from your manager - you are the manager. Be motivated in all aspects of the digital nomad lifestyle, as you wanted to work in this way, you need to show you have the drive to pull it off.

There are several reasons that motivation is particularly important when you're working with clients, and the first, most important one is to show them that you have a passion for what you're doing. This is especially important in the inquiry phase, highlighting to clients that you aren't somebody who is so laid back he/she's horizontal. You're active, motivated and ready to take on new challenges - make sure it comes across in your communication.

With a lack of motivation, digital nomads will struggle to complete projects on time or even reply to messages (the simplest task in the whole digital nomad lifestyle). You don't need anybody to point out just how severe it would be to not complete a project on time.

In case you need it laid out right in front of you, it can lead to cancellations and/or the breakdown in the seller/client relationship, which basically means they'll never work with you again.

> *"With a lack of motivation, digital nomads will struggle to complete projects on time, or even reply to messages..."*

Another key point relating to a lack of motivation is that you'll find it much harder to pick projects up, and you'll find yourself wanting to put down the ones you're currently working on so easily. Without the drive to persevere with your projects, you'll never make any significant progress.

> *"Without the drive to persevere with your projects, you'll never make any significant progress".*

It can be tempting to stay in bed all day or get distracted by things around you and this is another important reason why you need to master self-motivation. Before working as a digital nomad, you may not have been subjected to distractions such as Netflix, online shopping or going to the bar, so you have to learn how to manage that.

Stay motivated, get your work done on time, every time and always present yourself as the passionate hard-working person you want to be. That's a golden rule in freelancing, so don't forget it.

Take a More Human Approach

Always ensure that your communication isn't too clear-cut and corporate. You're not a permanent employee of the company or individual you're completing a project for. By no means should you be disrespectful or say anything that may be deemed inappropriate, but it means you should aim to be more personable, showing a bit more of who you really are.

Taking a more human approach, offering a more conversational tone in your communication allows people to warm to you much faster than they would in a more corporate setting. Remember this isn't your conventional nine to five, you've got a much shorter window to show people the kind of person you are.

With that in mind, always consider how you're representing yourself and judge it based on the environment you're in. If the people you're working for are very clear-cut and corporate, it may not be the direction to go in, but if it's a more pleasant environment then definitely consider the points brought forward here. Let your personality shine through, providing it's all positive.

> *"Let your personality shine through, providing it's all positive".*

HOW TO FIND WORK

Okay, so we've talked about the various aspects of the digital nomad lifestyle that you may not already have been aware of and the many things you should expect from choosing a career path like this. What we haven't yet discussed is where exactly you might find this work across the world that we've been speaking of so much.

Especially when you're starting out as a digital nomad, the path you're about to take isn't as clear as those who have been in the game for months, years, if not decades. That said, it's my hope that this guide can provide you with an insight that most established digital nomads didn't have back when they first started working this way. I want to make it easier for you to not only survive but thrive.

In this chapter, I'll explain just some of the many options available to a digital nomad when it comes to the remote working world, as right now I imagine it feels very daunting for you if you're just starting out. With this guide, there's no need to be afraid of what the future holds. A sea of opportunities awaits, and this is where things get exciting.

The world of remote working, miles apart from the conventional nine to five is full of exciting opportunities but unfortunately, just as many scams. It's very tricky to know who you should believe, if the job you're about to take is genuine or if you're just wasting your valuable time for nothing.

> *"The world of remote working, miles apart from the conventional nine to five is full of exciting opportunities but unfortunately, just as many scams".*

Firstly, let's take a look at the different types of remote jobs available to you when you're entering the wonderful world of being a digital nomad.

Freelance

One of the most popular options, freelancing gives you the freedom to pick and choose from the available jobs out there, often being able to pick what you feel you'd enjoy the most. If you want, you can take on multiple projects at the same time and flit between projects whilst making a nice bit of money.

Best of all, freelancing comes with the freedom to choose your own holiday days, and if there's an emergency in your personal life, there's no manager to turn to when you need time off. You can just go. You're your own manager in every sense with this way of working.

The trouble with freelancing is that often the jobs pay very little, unless you can find the right client, or they find you. Many freelancing websites in particular consist of just as many, if not more everyday people as business professionals. Therefore, finding somebody who is willing to pay what you're worth per hour can be very tricky.

You will too often find that on those particular websites, many are offering what you can do but much cheaper, and though they would get a quality product with you, many customers simply see the bottom line and unfortunately go for the cheapest option.

That isn't to say that freelancing options won't work out for you, but very often it can take quite some time to build up your profile and rise through the ranks of your competitors, particularly if they're doing what you can do but cheaper. Regardless, it's still a worthwhile option that should definitely be considered.

Contract

Contract work can be very lucrative but unfortunately does drag you back to the 'conventional nine to five' element of your old life. Back to a normal working week, but this time potentially in a different country, state or city, so it still can be exciting.

Contract work is often much harder to come across, as many companies rely on recommendations for potential contract candidates, and if you're not as established as somebody who already does what you can do, you'd better hope you're cheaper.

A key bonus of contract work is that you're effectively treated as if you're a permanent member of staff (for the short time you're actually there of course). You'll likely receive all the same staff benefits that the rest of the team is getting, and you may even be eligible for scheduled bonuses (and other rewards/incentives) depending on the contract they offer you.

Starting a Business

Some people believe that the only way you can truly achieve freedom when working is to start your own company, not only being your own manager but being your own boss. This way you truly can be in control of your time, money and career.

The only trouble with starting your own business is that in reality, there's far more to it than being your own boss, and you wouldn't believe how much managers actually rely on other people for. Being a manager is difficult, particularly if the processes of running a business are very new to you.

This is an option for those who are serious about taking something from concept to reality, rather than just having a service to offer. You need to be forward-thinking, be able to think on your feet and be driven in business. If you don't have the drive for it, it's simply not for you. Starting a business typically isn't for most people either and that's fine. You can make money from your skills by exploring a different option.

Platforms for Jobs/Projects

Fiverr

Fiverr is one of the world's leading freelancing job websites, with users from across the globe and hundreds of thousands of orders being placed each day. It's clear to see that Fiverr is working for 'sellers' (freelancers) and buyers alike.

Though many people are looking to get their jobs commissioned for very small fees and time-wasters are rife, there's a lot to love about Fiverr. A simple vetting process and clear, effective brief taking can often determine whether or not a buyer is really serious about the services you have to offer.

But before we get into all that, let's first explore the processes of the website. Before you can do anything on Fiverr, you must first set up an account, detailing who you are, what your strengths are, your educational background and your previous experience.

You'll then need to create 'gigs', which are essentially the services you wish to offer; for instance, "I will design your logo" would be a key example of a gig title on Fiverr.

Effectively describing what you will do, followed by the cost you wish to charge for it.

A useful tip when creating a gig is to ensure you implement SEO practices. Fiverr uses algorithms and rankings which can be measured through analytics on your seller dashboard.

From there, you can either 'apply' for open gig requests that are posted by potential buyers (these are usually posted at scarily low rates that wouldn't be worth your time at all), or you can wait for potential buyers to come to you directly. This can often take some time, particularly if you're very new to the website.

Buyers can also sometimes be initially wary of somebody who doesn't have any feedback. Another useful tip here is to get some friends and family to sign up, purchase your gig and leave a review. This way you stand out to potential clients.

It may be a good idea if you choose to use Fiverr that you take on one or two very small, very cheap jobs just to get some quick feedback. Good feedback, even in small quantities, will spur on other potential customers to at least message you, if not place an order. The more feedback you have, the better.

> *"The more feedback you have, the better".*

Many people have found success on Fiverr and Fiverr themselves have even used blog posts to inform their sellers of 'when it's the right moment to quit your job and focus on Fiverr', so it's clearly paying off for many members. There is a lot of money to be made on Fiverr if you can find the right clients. It just takes time and you need to be patient, but you can be working with people from across the world, even if you don't get to go and work in their fancy offices abroad.

My advice would be not to focus on Fiverr as a main source of income unless you are making enough money every single month from your gigs and they are categories that will always be used. I only use Fiverr as a side income as rates are extremely low from other freelancers which means that those of us providing high-quality work cannot compete with the low prices.

There is also the opportunity to be offered further work outside of Fiverr if a client likes your work. Although this is something to take extreme caution with, it is possible.

Important Notes

A fee of 20% applies to your payments for using the platform.

Create the maximum number of 6 gigs even if they are similar; Fiverr likes this, and you will be shown to more potential clients.

Never take payments or work for a new client outside of Fiverr.

It can take months to get your first gig, so this is no get rich quick scheme.

Take the time in creating your profile, create videos for your gig if possible and every month to two months just alter each gig slightly.

Start out with low prices to encourage clients than when you have feedback of around 10 clients, increase your prices.

There is an "out of office" function on there if you don't want to take gigs or are on holiday.
Set reasonable delivery dates; if you get an order when you least expect it and you have set a delivery date of 1 day; you will become stuck.

Never extend your delivery date and give excuses to clients. It doesn't look good.

Your response rate is vital, reply to messages as soon as you can.

Upwork

Upwork is probably the largest freelancing website out there right now, and if you're looking to work remotely as a self-proclaimed digital nomad, you should be all over this website. Whilst Upwork does have similarities to Fiverr the one main difference is that you apply for the projects on Upwork.

Again, like Fiverr, it operates under the same kind of principles. There are thousands of jobs posted each day and even more orders placed than there are with Fiverr. Many people have found success with Upwork, providing a regular stream of income for many digital nomads across the world.

Much like Fiverr, it, of course, takes a while to build up your profile and get people trusting you. Feedback is king in the freelance game and a good track record is almost a necessity before a client will even consider placing an order with you, which is difficult if you're very new to the website.

As I said regarding Fiverr, Upwork is much the same, where I'd recommend you take a few quick and easy jobs just to get some good feedback on your profile. You wouldn't believe how much better it makes you look to potential buyers; it seems to put them at ease when they're considering booking you for a job.

Many people say that the key to becoming successful on Upwork is to have a cover letter that really stands out. Use the cover letter as your opportunity to say exactly why you think you're the person for the job and what you can bring to the project that nobody else could. Once you've got the hang of writing a killer cover letter, you're on to a winner.

Important Notes

Create a profile with an SEO focus, it is vital to include all your skills.

You can create 2 specialised profiles which should be a focus on your strongest skills. For example, have your main profile outlining everything and then a profile for SEO writing and one for Logo design.

You have to purchase "connects" in order to apply for jobs on Upwork. Prices vary dependant on your country, and it could be anywhere from 2 – 6 connects for a job.

When you search for a job, always stick to the first 2 pages with the newest jobs. I have found the highest success rate doing this as clients will see your proposal immediately which can be vital if they are in need of a freelancer urgently.
Never take work outside of Upwork and NEVER do unpaid trials.

Be aware that for longer projects on Upwork, your screen will be recorded, and all actions logged. So, no watching Netflix whilst working.

You will be charged fees based on how much you earn on a per-client basis.

There are other sites out there but the two that I have listed are the most profitable for freelancers. There are also websites where you can apply for remote jobs with companies. I will go through some excellent sites and also give a list of some others you can use.

WeWorkRemotely

WeWorkRemotely is great for everybody from content writers to graphic designers. There is a vast pool of jobs available to creative, ambitious, and innovative digital nomads who want to generate a more stable source of income.

You will find a one-page site that lists a variety of remote jobs in date order and under their respective categories. You can read job descriptions and hit the links to apply directly on the company's website, and it's that simple.

There are no fees or profiles involved with this website and you will be relying on your cover letter, CV and application form for success. Pay particular attention to your cover letter, employers are more interested in a unique cover letter than a standard CV.

There are hundreds of websites out there for remote jobs and there will likely be an increase in these sites over the next 5 years. At the end of this book, I will provide a list of resources that you can use.

When it comes to the freelancing website options I've pointed out in this chapter, it may be a good idea to consider (if this is the direction you're looking to pursue) the possibility of creating accounts across all of them. This would be a good point to highlight that there are also many other freelancing websites out there too. But, using a combination of multiple freelancing platforms, providing you can effectively manage them and the admin that comes with them could be useful - and lucrative.

Especially when you're first starting out and it's taking time for any good money to come through, at least if you have accounts across multiple platforms, you're building to something good at a much quicker rate. Even in those early, quieter days, you can still be taking on at least a few small jobs to get you by until the bigger stuff comes.

Though that's just an idea, and it's important to point out that it may not work for you. You may find that you wish to push all your attention on just one freelancing website and that's fine. It all depends on how you work best, whether you think you can manage multiple platforms, or you'd rather have a focus site.

With having a focus site, you can drive the success of your account on just one platform. We all work differently, and as long as it's working for you then it's all good.

> *"We all work differently, and as long as it's working for you then it's all good".*

I hope this chapter has given you an insight into the many options you have available to you as a digital nomad. There are many opportunities in the list above that will allow you to travel the world, meet new people, work remotely from the comfort of your own accommodation (if that works for you) and so many other things outside of the conventional nine to five routine.

The trick is to always go into this with an open mind and being open to trying a freelancing website even if you don't think it's the best way for you, as you never really know until you live the life of a digital nomad. We all get things wrong and I'd hate for you to miss out on a great opportunity just because you assumed it was the wrong move to make. Experimentation is key for a digital nomad.

"Experimentation is key for a digital nomad".

PROBLEMS TO PREPARE FOR

Though we've pretty much covered the entirety of the negative side of life as a digital nomad, I feel it's important to reiterate certain points and get you thinking about ways in which you can combat these issues. Regardless of what you may believe, it is inevitable that you will encounter problems during your freelance journey.

Of course, you'll notice certain topics come up at different points within this guide, but it's important to note that I'm not structuring this guide in this way just to get alarm bells ringing. I simply hope you take the advice I wish I would have been given years ago when I was entering the big bad world (the world that's frightening but full of exciting opportunities).

Firstly, let's start with the newer topics we're yet to fully flesh out in this document. Now, you could sit and worry all day about the problems and risks involved with life as a digital nomad, but that wouldn't get you anywhere. That's why I'm going to provide you with the problems and hopefully give you direction in how you can move forward, and hopefully prevent it happening altogether.

Negative Feedback

It's the last thing a digital nomad wants to see or hear. Negative feedback on work you've put valuable time into can be earth-shattering, particularly if you're relying heavily on the money from that job - as, with bad feedback, you might not be getting paid (this is something we'll cover in this chapter in further detail). Negative feedback can also have lasting damage to your freelancing profiles on the internet.

Firstly, let's discuss the effects that negative feedback can have on your mental health, as this is a subject that often gets very little airtime when it comes to the media's coverage of digital nomads and the lives of freelancers. When you think about the loneliness, rejection, and risk of bad feedback involved in the life of a digital nomad, it's easy for this to become too much for even the strongest of us.

Mental health is an important matter for us to discuss, particularly when you're living this lifestyle outside of the 'norm'. It's easy to think you're out of the loop with society and if you receive bad feedback, that you're just not good enough.

When you receive bad feedback, it's important not to take it to heart, as it really is just business, and should only ever be treated as such. It's hard to distance your emotions from it, I understand; particularly if you're relying on that money to pay for your necessities.

It's crucial that when you're in this position, that you remember how it's just a business transaction at the end of the day, and you need to come away from that situation having presented yourself in the best possible light, having tried to resolve the situation in some way.

"How can I avoid negative feedback?" is a common question I am asked. Well, the simple answer would be that you need to make your work as strong as possible and do your very best to 'wow' the client. If that means going above and beyond the call of duty then by all means, go for it. However, it's important to also consider that particularly on freelancing websites, there is a lot of time wasters who are out to see what they can get for nothing.

Unfortunately, the freelancing websites are often in favour of the buyer, rather than the seller (you), which means that if a client doesn't want to pay because they have a negative opinion of your work, then the transaction can be cancelled and the buyer doesn't need to pay. This opens the floodgates for potential scammers who wish to try their luck at getting some free work.

One point that I will stress more than any other is that "every client is different". No matter how good your work is there will always be someone in the world that hates it, whilst that may sound harsh, it is unfortunately true. If you come across a client that hates your work and you feel as though you went above and beyond, my advice would be to cancel the work and retract the contract to avoid negative feedback. If this is not an option, reply to the client and ask them to cancel the contract as you feel the partnership on the project in question will not work out.

Client Doesn't Want to Pay

Having covered this to a certain extent in the previous segment, it's important to always consider the possibility that your client may not want to pay for the work you do, and that's exactly why you should never 'spend' until you actually have the money for the job in your hand.

The best way of combating the likelihood of a client not wanting to pay is to put your heart and soul into the work, no matter how much the client is spending. You should go above and beyond all expectations in an attempt to please your client, especially because this can form the roots of a budding relationship between yourself and the client; thus, potentially leading to more work.

In order to prevent the client saying they're not going to pay is to first fully understand their wants and needs from you regarding the project, doing everything you possibly can to ensure you're not going to let them down, within the agreements that you set out at the start of the project.

You almost need to put in a kind of vetting process in order to filter the time-wasters from the genuine buyers on these sites, particularly as it's so easy for just anybody to make a profile - and if they want, exploit you. As I mentioned, freelancing websites are often always in favour of the buyer and unfortunately, the seller is left to pick up the pieces if a transaction goes wrong.

You should also consider putting some money aside from each successful job you carry out, as that way you always have a bit of money to dip into if you ever experience a tricky customer who refuses to pay. It's bound to happen from time to time, it's just unfortunate and can be devastating if you're relying on the money.

Do everything you can to prevent it; prepare for the first but expect the best. Have both a positive and realistic attitude when it comes to your new life as a digital nomad and you'll be fine.

Whilst there are certain levels of protection when you work on freelancing sites, there is practically no protection when you work directly with a client. That is why if you are really wanting to protect yourself, you should draw up a contract or ask the client to do so.

Obviously, if you are applying for a project through a website you will always have some form of contract to sign, but if you verbally agree on a project with a client then you should discuss the possibility of a signed document.

Administration

Probably the most mundane problem on this list, that also probably doesn't make for the most exciting reading (so, I'll apologise now). Particularly if you're choosing to go in the direction of a fully-fledged digital nomad from a previous life of 'conventional nine to five', it can be hard to adjust to one simple rule - you need to do your own admin now.

It's so easy to forget that if you've come from a conventional office environment where you can rely on your department's receptionist or office administration team to cover that side of things. There's also nobody to remind you of your schedule, so it's key that you're always on top of things and know exactly what your next task at hand is.

Another key element of administration is inquiries - equally as important as organising, maintaining and checking your schedule, as inquiries can lead to jobs. It's crucial that you try to respond to all inquiries as efficiently as possible and turn as many of those serious inquiries into new orders.

This is particularly important to remember if you're active on multiple different freelancing websites, as your admin is at least twice as hard to keep up with. Regularly check your inbox and avoid missing out on potential sales, your wallet will thank you later when it's nice and full.

Social Life

Let's be blunt about this, as there's no skating around this issue, your social life is going to now suffer because of the working lifestyle you have chosen. It's outside of the norm, and unless all of your friends are now digital nomads too, it's going to be easy to feel like you've slipped out of the loop with everything.

This can be disheartening, particularly if you're struggling to find much work and you're striving to find leads. It's one thing being successful and losing contact with your friendship group, but to fall out of the loop and have no money is just a tragedy.

It's therefore important that for your own sanity, and the good of your relationship with your friendship circle that even if you're snowed under when you find a minute you should definitely touch base. It goes without saying that you should take an interest in what they are doing and if need be, apologise for being distant since you've taken up your new digital nomad lifestyle.

Your social life shouldn't have to suffer because of your work, but in the life of a digital nomad, it's unfortunately inevitable that from time to time you're going to miss social events. Just do your very best not to miss the important ones. It's important that while you're trying to be a successful digital nomad, you should also still want to be a good friend.

It's possible to be a successful digital nomad and a good friend, it's just all about finding the right balance. Do everything you can to survive and thrive as a digital nomad and make sure to check in with your friends, after all, you need them just like they need you.

> *"It's possible to be a successful digital nomad and a good friend, it's just all about finding the right balance".*

When you don't find the right balance, it can be easy for your new way of working life to cause friction within your friendship group. It's important to remember that not everybody will be wholly supportive of your new career choice, but do your best to make them understand, and do your best to be a good friend. As I said, it's just all about finding that balance.

IMPORTANT THINGS TO CONSIDER

There are many things you should consider before ultimately making the choice of whether or not the life of a digital nomad is for you. After all, it's a very difficult decision to make, as there can be some drawbacks which are deciding factors for you.

Ultimately, it's all about finding what is best for you and finding a sustainable way of living that brings you the success you desire.

There are many things I've included on this list that are so obvious, you've probably completely overlooked them. It's my hope that with this chapter, you'll be able to collect all the information presented and take it away in order to make an informed decision on whether or not the digital nomad lifestyle is for you, and if it is, what you need to do now.

Your Previous Job

It may seem so obvious and you've probably thought about this a thousand times over, but you can guarantee that at least one person reading this hasn't actually judged the digital nomad lifestyle against his/her previous experience.

Before you can even comprehend what the future holds for you as an emerging digital nomad, you first need to compare everything you've learned in this guide against what you've done up to this point. Think of what it is about your previous/current job that has influenced your decision in picking up and reading this guide.

Then consider how things would be different if you were your own 'manager' and the world was your office. If it doesn't sound like a preferable option, then you may need to reconsider this particular career change…

It might be a useful exercise to think about your previous/current job right now. Chances are, you have bigger picture ideas that don't quite suit what you're doing now, and that's one of your main reasons for wanting to get out. It's also likely you're feeling trapped, particularly if you're in a conventional office environment working a nine to five job with a manager breathing down your neck at any given moment.

No matter the reason you're looking for the exit door, it's worthwhile to do this exercise. Pinpoint the most influential reasons that you're reading this guide and considering a new way of working life and then think realistically about just how different life as a digital nomad would be.

Use this information to create a 'benefits and drawbacks' graph. It will help you to put things into perspective and give you a clearer picture of the right move to make for your future. When you're finished, count how many benefits you have in comparison to drawbacks.

If you've got far more benefits then great, it sounds like you're on the right track. However, if you're finding that there are more drawbacks on your list than anything else, you possibly need to reconsider your next move. It's all about making the right, well-informed decision for you, using all the resources available to you in order to make your decision.

What Kind of Person You Are

The life of a digital nomad isn't for the faint-hearted, as you've probably guessed by this point. It can be a life of financial instability (at least at first), unimaginable stress when the pressure is on and at times, it can be a life of loneliness. It's unfortunate to describe the digital nomad lifestyle in this way, but as I've said throughout this guide, I want to be real with you, my readers, and I will never feed you an unrealistic dream.

Don't get me wrong, the lifestyle of a digital nomad can also be a flourishing one, with many wonderful and lucrative opportunities - it's certainly not all doom and gloom, and I'd never want you to believe it was. But it requires hard, constant work in order for even a chance at success. And you need to be strong-willed.

This way of life isn't for everybody, so a key piece of advice I would offer is that you evaluate and then re-evaluate your choice to become a digital nomad and transform your lifestyle in the process.

I'm not saying you won't be able to hack it, but you need to be certain that there's 'digital nomad' in your DNA. You need to know that you've got the strength, motivation, determination and thick skin to deal with all the different kinds of situations that will be thrown at you when you enter your new life as a digital nomad.

"So, how do I judge if I'm right for this way of life?" you may be asking yourself. I would suggest that you have two ways forward at this point. You can ask your friends, family, and colleagues to be blunt with you, ask them to tell you how it is and give their honest, constructive feedback on what kind of person you are. If they're telling you that you're emotional and fragile then it's possible that the life of a digital nomad may be too much for you.

If, however, you're hearing that people think you're strong-willed, motivated and adaptable, you're probably onto a winner. You're probably the perfect fit for the life of a digital nomad.

Another thing you can do is look for answers from within. It sounds cheesy but I don't intend for it to be, rather you should always look to self-evaluate; judging yourself based on the 'person specification' for a digital nomad.

Do you think you fit the bill for the job?

If you're having doubts this early on, then it requires some serious thought before you continue any further with the process.

Taxes

This is something we will cover in more depth in a later chapter, but you need to consider that when you're following the life of a digital nomad. You're not just responsible for your own admin - you have to sort your own taxes too!

For some digital nomads, this is what makes it all feel real, like you're completely in control of your life, your working life and the way you manage it and more importantly, your finances. With great power comes great responsibility… it can be an exciting yet daunting task.

Ensuring your tax documents and your financial records are up to date, accurate and clear is one of the most important (if boring) aspects of being a digital nomad. You can no longer rely on the safety blanket of a regular monthly salary coming in, now you don't have a fixed income each month, your taxes are going to be complicated.

As I mentioned, in the UK you should expect to pay income tax based on your profits, so it's important you know your numbers. You'll need to know exactly what your profits are month on month, year on year in order to be charged the correct tax rates.

Financial advisors and other such services are available, and this is something I will cover in a future chapter. Just remember, always do your taxes and do them right - it's a golden rule of being a digital nomad.

ORGANISATION

As you should already expect, when you're your own manager in the lifestyle of a digital nomad, you need to be on the ball and your organisational skills need to be on top form. When you're just one person, it's understandable that it can be difficult to manage your admin on top of all the projects you're taking on but somehow, you need to find a way of accomplishing it.

Now, there's no reason to sell you on something that just won't happen, so I won't. Nobody is going to help you out, at least not for free anyway. Most likely, there's no chance that you're going to be able to afford an assistant or receptionist. That would be the dream though, right? Luckily, there are ways you can effectively self-manage and further develop your organisational skills to where they need to be in order to not only survive as a digital nomad but thrive.

"Luckily, there are ways you can effectively self-

> *manage and further develop your organisational skills to where they need to be..."*

After all, the last thing you want to do is miss deadlines, disappoint clients and risk potential bad reviews which will only deter other potential clients from hiring you for your services. Effective, efficient utilisation of your organisation skills, encouraging your own personal development, you will be well on track to lead a successful freelancing career and encourage clients to come back for more.

In this chapter, we'll take a look at the various tools at your disposal in order to not only develop your organisational skills but to then maintain them, so you never miss a deadline and keep everybody involved in the process happy and smiling.

Let's take a look at the various methods you can implement. Some you may find obvious and some may be new to you, but all are useful. With that said, it's all about finding what works for you and we all need varying degrees of help in this department.

To-do Lists

The first, most obvious solution to keep track of your tasks and improve your organisational skills is to implement the use of to-do lists. Allowing you to make note of your daily, weekly and monthly tasks as well as any one-off things you may need to do. Basically, if you have a job to do, you best hope you've written it on your to-do list, or this method just won't work. Admittedly, it requires preparation, but that's how to stay organised and keep customers happy.

By successfully implementing a to-do list, you'll never miss a task again. You can even go one step further by marking them under varying levels of importance, with the ones with the shortest deadlines being the ones with more urgency. If it helps you to process the information faster and easier, consider using colour codes.

As I mentioned, it's all about finding what works for you in order for you to ensure you keep your clients happy and get those glowing reviews coming in. Take it one step further and use a whiteboard to keep track of your goals so they are always visible.

Calendars

Particularly in the digital age of today, calendars can be perfect for giving reminders in short, easy to digest bursts of information at the vibration of a smartphone. Especially when utilised on your smartphone, calendar information can be brought to you wherever you are in the world. You no longer need to be sat at a computer to check it.

On all smartphone calendars of today, you can set as many reminders as you need to and even set reminders on top of reminders. For instance, you can set a single reminder to keep popping up every five minutes until you action it and check it off.

"Particularly in the digital age of today, calendars can be perfect for giving reminders in short, easy to digest bursts of information at the vibration of a smartphone".

Project Management Software

Project management software can admittedly first appear complicated, but if you're willing to put the work into getting your head around it, you'll give yourself the best chance for success.

There are various free project management software options - with many available on hand-held devices that are also very easy to use. Project management software allows you to list every job you have on the go, with information on the tasks within that project you need to complete and when you need to complete them.

Setting subtasks on smartphone applications and software such as this can further increase your efficiency and ensure you're at the top of your game, on the ball and never scrambling at the last minute to get jobs done - as this will only risk the quality of the work you're producing.

Some notable and essentially "free" project management platforms include Asana and Trello. There are many others out there and if this is the way you want to stay organised then test out whichever one works best for your needs.

Distraction-Free Zones

Though it's not exactly a method of improving your organisational skills, as it's not a tangible product, working in a distraction-free zone will further increase your efficiency and ensure you're working with those deadlines in mind.

With more focus, you're never going to forget those deadlines anyway and you're always going to give yourself enough time to complete the work.

Let's say you started to work in a distraction-free zone and utilised the benefits of maintaining a constant to-do list, you're going to be the most organised version of yourself you can be.

> *"...working in a distraction-free zone will further increase your efficiency and ensure you're working with those deadlines in mind".*

At the end of the day, it's all about ensuring you keep the client happy and ensure the quality is high. The only way you can do this is by ensuring you're not working right up to the very last minute before the deadline.

As you now know, a perfect way of avoiding these kinds of situations is by improving your organisational skills. Luckily, you can always refer back to the information presented to you in this chapter.

MONEY & TAXES

Everything always comes back to money, I know. But when you're living the life of a digital nomad, your money is more important than ever before, and the taxman will want to know where it has come from. It's my hope that with this chapter, I can give you the guidance you're looking for when it comes to the money you're earning and how to approach your tax situation.

After all, I understand just how daunting it can be when you're looking at tax information requirements and not having a clue what to do next. It all feels very 'grown- up' and it will probably make you feel so far out of your depth that you'll want to bury your head in the sand (or your work) and avoid the boring, complicated question of asking for help.

I want to make everything regarding your money and taxes easier. Mostly because I understand just how difficult it is to successfully manage your lifestyle as a digital nomad as it is, without having to worry about learning the complexities around incoming revenues and what it means when it comes to your tax.

So, without further ado, let's take a more in-depth look and make this clearer in your head for the good of everybody.

Taxes for freelancers are different in most countries, as different areas will require you to hit different minimum amounts before you are charged tax. In the United States, if you earn $400 or more from freelance work within the period of one year, you are responsible for paying the self-employment tax of 15.3%. This tax solely exists to cover your Social Security and Medicare taxes. Also, if you reside in the United States, you will likely pay federal, state and local taxes.

In the UK, as a freelancer, your income tax and National Insurance is calculated based on your projected profits. First, if you haven't already then you need to register with HMRC to tell them you're 'self-employed' and you will be reminded that the tax year in the UK runs from April to April the following year.

In the UK, you can earn up to £12,500 (as of the date of this publication) before you are charged any tax. This is because tax breaks are in place in order to ensure the system doesn't unfairly treat those freelancers/self-employed members of the community who aren't doing particularly well financially year on year.

It's important to highlight that the £12,500 figure is simply a standard personal allowance figure, and this may vary depending on the person, their background and their current expenditure.

It's important to note that your National Insurance payments when working in a self- employed capacity are being used for good, not just 'so the man can pocket your money'. Your National Insurance payments are used for State Pension and Universal Credit.

There is so much information on the internet regarding all of this and many official council and government websites now have easy to follow, interactive questionnaires in order to point you in the right direction if you become stuck and it's unclear what to do next. I would always recommend checking with somebody, even if you're 99% certain that you've got it all right the first time. Check you've got the facts, then rest easy.

It's important to always check that you're paying the right tax and if you have questions that you can't find anywhere on the internet, always seek the advice and assistance of a financial professional - citizens advice (or other alike services) often offers advice like this free of charge and it can be particularly beneficial when you're just starting out.

Each country has its own rules, regulations, and requirements when it comes to tax and there is no way it could be effectively covered for every territory in just this one guide, if it could, it would end up being a very long document!

I would strongly advise that you hire an accountant when working as a freelancer, you can generally find a good service for a reasonable price. I would estimate that in the UK, a good fee for an accountant would be between £350-£550. Of course, you don't have to spend money on an accountant but filing your own taxes is incredibly difficult. If you choose a good accountant, they will do their best to actually save you money on your taxes.

A part of your taxes relies on keeping track of your expenses and income throughout the year. Working as a freelancer it is likely you could receive income through several different sources, for example, PayPal, Stripe, bank account and many others. You should create a spreadsheet to record all of this information accurately and I would advise that as soon as an action has taken place, you record it. When I say action, I am referring to payment, expense or anything that needs to be financially recorded for tax purposes.

Expenses are another important factor of your taxes as they will save you money by reducing the amount you owe. Anything you spend that is related to your work or business is considered an expense.

For example, if you buy a sim card abroad for data that you use to work on, that is an expense, or if you pay for someone to create a logo for you, that is also an expense. If you are unsure of what constitutes as an expense, then you should consult with your accountant.

PREPARING FOR YOUR FUTURE

When we're speaking about the life of a digital nomad like it's just as normal as a 'conventional nine to five' job, it's easy to forget that it's such a serious, important decision to choose that path. At the end of the day, this is your future and it really can go one of two ways (as unfortunate as it is to say that). Let's think positively for a second. Your future can be just as bright, if not brighter than somebody in a conventional nine to five. You just need to prepare.

Your future as a digital nomad and your future as a functioning, healthy member of society is right now unclear, as you're just starting out in your journey and nobody knows what the future will hold. By no means do I mean it's going to be hard for you to survive in this world, I simply believe your future is just going to be much different from that of somebody in a conventional nine to five office job.

"How do I prepare for what comes next?" is probably a question you've asked yourself many times before reading this guide and even at points in this guide, but I firmly believe this is a question you should be asking yourself regularly. Nobody knows exactly what their best next move is, as we're all different. Our situations are all different and as I said, nobody can predict the future. That doesn't mean you can't do the right preparation in order to get ready for any eventuality.

Nowhere to Call Home

Your future isn't going to be getting up at 7 am and eating breakfast before commuting to work and then at 5 pm travelling back home. You're likely not going to have the same kind of structure that many of your friends and family currently have.

You're going to be living somewhat outside of the norm; your schedule will be different; your social hours will be all over the place and you'll likely not have anywhere you can really call 'home'. It can be a lot to take in for even the best of us - that's something you have to prepare for.

It's important if cliché to point out that your home is where your heart is, and your heart is likely to be where your friends and family are which can be difficult if they're hundreds, if not thousands of miles away. Remember that your friends and family are just a phone call away, no matter where you are in the world.

I know we've talked about loneliness in this guide already, but we've not mentioned the sense of being homesick yet and that's equally just as important. Prepare to feel like this at some point, as you begin your journey as a digital nomad, as in your future in this way of working life, you're definitely going to experience it.

Children & Mortgages

Your friends may be settling down around you, but if you're living the life of a digital nomad then you're likely to be either travelling the world and working on various cool projects or busy working remotely on freelancing websites. It's likely that when you're living this kind of lifestyle that you'll put your personal life on hold, at least while you get going and start getting money coming through.

Though this isn't always the case and if you're willing to put the work in and be as flexible as possible, you can manage parenthood and your digital nomad life together, it's just a very careful balance that you need to strike in order to get it right. If you do find yourself in this situation, you'll find many obstacles in your path and you'll likely trip up at least once or twice, but do not let this deter you if the life of a digital nomad is what you seriously want, fight for it whilst not forgetting your responsibilities as a parent.

Saving Money

Saving money is quite possibly the most difficult thing for a digital nomad. No longer in the confines of a conventional nine to five office job, that is admittedly dull but provided a regular, stable income, things are much different. There are many reasons you may want to save money, but in this segment, we'll just focus on a few of the key reasons.

Firstly, save money for your future; for when you want that modern apartment or that flashy sports car, whatever it may be you're saving for, you'll certainly find it hard when you don't really know how much you might be earning in any particular month.

It's important to remember to save what you feel most comfortable with and not to 'break your back', so to speak. The simplest way of looking at it is to consider your expenditures for the month, judge how much money you'll have to cover those costs and then go from there. I would probably say it would be unrealistic to save more than 25% of your income as it may hinder you until your next payslip comes through.

Another reason you may be saving is that you suspect there may be a dry spell coming, where the work stops coming through and you face financial difficulty. This is the most responsible form of saving for the future, and I would always recommend you try and do this in some way if you can. Saving for the dry spells isn't preparing to fail, rather it's preparing for the worst, just in case. It's simply sensible.

It would be foolish of somebody to say or believe that they'll never experience a dry spell, as nobody can predict the future and arrogance will get you nowhere in the digital nomad world. It's in your best interest to have money to fall back on. It's in your best interest to plan for your future - good or bad.

> *"Saving for the dry spells isn't preparing to fail, rather it's preparing for the worst, just in case. It's simply sensible".*

As a final message in this chapter, though it's crucial to be good with your money, particularly when you're in the potentially financially unstable life of a digital nomad, it's also important to have fun. Never forget who you are and what makes you happy. It's like the rule from the 2009 film Zombieland, "Enjoy the little things". That goes for all walks of life, no matter what situation you in, we all need some enjoyment to get us through the rough patches.

It might not seem like you should, but we all need a bit of retail therapy (in some form) every now and then - whether it's treating yourself to some new clothes or having an evening out at the theatre. After you've been working so hard, you most definitely deserve it. Enjoy the little things but be sensible with your money for the most part.

> *"Enjoy the little things but be sensible with your money for the most part".*

YOUR FIRST CLIENT

When you've finally set up all your freelancing profiles and you've spread the word about the services you offer, all that's left is to wait for the inquiries to come rolling in. You may get many, you may get none for quite some time - everybody has different experiences when they first start out and it all depends on the services you're offering and what the current marketplace is like at the point of you entering it.

This chapter exists to give you a clearer insight into what to expect from your first experience with a client. It could go swimmingly, or it could go horrendously wrong; at the end of the day, your fate rests in your hands and will depend on just how prepared you are for it and how motivated you are to excel.

> *"It could go swimmingly, or it could go horrendously wrong; at the end of the day, your fate rests in your hands..."*

What to Expect

The first experience every freelancer has is different and if we were to list every possible thing you should look to expect, this book itself could take out an entire forest in paper. You should expect to feel out of your depth more than anything else, but everybody has to start somewhere, and you are likely more than capable of successfully carrying out the project you're about to undertake.

With a little positivity, motivation and a strong-willed attitude, you should expect to find your first project challenging, but not impossible. It's all about having the can-do attitude to please your first client (and all the ones that follow) and produce high-quality work, deserving of a glowing review.

> *"...you should expect to find your first project challenging, but not impossible".*

Problems

Let's start with the negatives and then work our way back to a resolution. This way, you're seeing just how badly it could go but then you're seeing how to avoid a situation where these problems arise. After all, it's certainly better to be aware of these various potential problems with your first client experience than it is to have it just happen and not even realise how it got to that point. Preparation is key in this game, so let's get into it.

The first, most obvious problem you may encounter is a client who is your polar opposite; somebody who has a completely different working style to you, somebody with a personality that clashes with your own and somebody who seems to want to make your working life hell. In this case, there is one thing you need to remember, they're working just like you are - it's business, it's not personal.

> *"The first, most obvious problem you may encounter is a client who is your polar opposite..."*

It's important to highlight that we're all only human; I understand you've read that phrase throughout this guide but it's key to understanding this potential situation, as you will at some point experience it anyway and know not to take things personally. At the end of the day, a problematic, polar opposite client just wants their job done in a very particular way, and you're getting paid to fulfill that need to a high standard.

The customer is always right, so do everything within reach to keep them happy and ensure you get paid and receive positive feedback on the job you do. Go into the process with the understanding that you're not here to make friends and neither are they, but you need to keep them happy.

Another problem you may encounter with your first client is not knowing how much information is the 'right' amount of information. It's a very tricky judgment to make. If you're looking at the brief you've been given for a particular project and you're wondering if it's a little slim, chances are that it probably is.

If there's any doubt in how you need to proceed with a project after reading the client's brief, then you need to request further clarification. There is no use in muddling your way through as that only opens you up to not completing the job how the client expected it to be done. Don't risk not getting paid, go back and check - there's absolutely no shame in it and the client will probably have more respect for you for it.

> *"If you're looking at the brief you've been given for a particular project and you're wondering if it's a little slim, chances are that it probably is".*

Finally, though it isn't the only other problem that you face (only the most common instances are going to be discussed in this chapter), you may feel a sense of vulnerability and a lack of confidence, unlike anything you've ever felt before. This is because this is the first time, you're actually putting yourself out there and actually now working within your digital nomad parameters for the first time. You may have so many possible outcomes swirling around your head that it's making you anxious and it's affecting your ability to effectively carry out the job.

Though it's going to be very difficult to do so, you need to put those thoughts and feelings to the back of your mind - as they're only going to distract you from the task at hand. Have the confidence to fight those thoughts and feelings and tell yourself that you are capable of doing a good job and you are right for the digital nomad lifestyle.

That's the only way you can overcome it.

Good Service

Good service is crucial if you're looking to expect a positive first client experience. Remember that you are the master of your own destiny and the fate of this project rests in your hands. There are several steps you can take to ensure a positive first client/project experience because after all, this will give you the confidence to continue with your digital nomad lifestyle, progress and ultimately succeed.

Firstly, you need to understand the importance of manners; speaking to each and every person you come into contact with, in a respectful, positive manner, ensuring they never feel like they're intruding on your day, or you are on theirs. Each and every client, and potential client needs to be treated as though they are valued because they should be. These people are sustaining the lifestyle you're trying to lead so make sure they know just how much you appreciate their custom.

Within the realms of treating your clients and potential clients with respect, you should also keep contact with them regularly, attempting to reply to their requests and inquiries within one hour where possible. The communication you have with your client is just important as the project itself, with both being the factors in which you will be judged come the completion of the project. It's just as 'make or break' as the quality of work you produce. Remember that.

Another step you should follow in order to ensure your first client experience is to implement sheer focus into the work you're producing. You need to be on the ball and willing to adapt in order to successfully complete the project to the highest standard you can possibly achieve. Avoid distractions that will only take you off course and affect the quality of work you produce, focus on client satisfaction with the hope it will lead to repeat business.

> "...focus on client satisfaction with the hope it will lead to repeat business".

On the subject of repeat business, it's never acceptable to treat any project as a one-off and go into it with the mindset of 'I won't work with them again anyway, so I'll rush through it' or anything to that effect. Always go into it with the mindset that the first project with a client is effectively your overall first impression with them, as it is. If it goes well, you may just get even more work - so do everything you can to push it in that direction.

Remember that the quality of your work and the way you treat your clients will be the deciding factors on whether or not the project was a success or a failure. If you're looking for a positive first client experience (you obviously are, who would want it to go badly?), you should definitely take everything from this chapter on board.

All in all, your first client experience could go one of two ways and you're not a fortune teller, so the best you can do is guide it in the best direction possible. Understand that you can't please everybody, but you can certainly try, in most cases, you'll find it works. You just need to be willing to put the work in.

> *"Understand that you can't please everybody, but you can certainly try, in most cases, you'll find it works".*

REVENUE STREAMS

I've talked about money throughout this guide on the digital nomad lifestyle, whether it's saving for your future or just how much you should expect to earn from this career path, but it's important to add to your knowledge and talk about revenue streams for a while.

It's powerful to note that all you need is a laptop and Wi-Fi and you can be making money from clients from across the world. But with that power comes revenue streams from multiple sources, and it can be hard to not only keep up with your schedule but to also keep track of how much money you have coming in. I'm not saying that you'll have so much money that you won't be able to keep up with where it's coming from, I'm simply saying it can be hard to know exactly what money you have come from which client, from which platform.

There are so many variables! You may have $200 coming in from Fiverr, $75 coming from Upwork, $100 coming from Outsourcely and various other random amounts from different websites.

It's therefore worth keeping a financial diary (this also helps when it comes to your taxes as you'll be able to accurately detail every job, how much it was worth and when you were paid for it. This financial diary/planner will give you a clearer picture of your revenue streams, how much money you should expect to make each month and if there are any payments you should be chasing.

> *"It's powerful to note that all you need is a laptop and Wi-Fi and you can be making money from clients across the world".*

On the point of payments, you should be chasing, this can be particularly tricky if you're dealing with many clients all at once, hence the importance of the financial diary and keeping on top of it. It's so easy to get flustered when you're living the life of a digital nomad but keeping on top of your finances should probably be your next priority after ensuring your work is the very best it can be. After all, you're doing all this to create a sustainable business and future.

Something we haven't yet talked about regarding the internet-based revenue streams and that is the fees. Most websites on the internet will charge a significant fee per completed sale you make on their website. This is effectively similar to what eBay would do if you sold an item with them, you're paying for them to 'host' the transaction.

Websites like Fiverr charge a large sum of 20%, which is large and does seem like a substantial chunk of your earnings, particularly if you're purely working from Fiverr (as it's a fifth of your salary gone).

However, when you really think about it, you'd be nowhere without the websites you're using, so just forget about the fee, get your head down and use the benefits of the platforms (millions of users, so millions of potential buyers) in order to make more money.

Revenue streams today are much different than they would have been even twenty years ago. We're now living in an age where we can fully benefit from the capabilities of the internet and earn money from clients across the world simply by using a digital device.

There are definitely more options available to digital nomads today than there were five years ago. The way of life continues to grow and develop, much like the technology we're using to enable that lifestyle. Revenue streams are available at the tap of a touch screen. It's that accessible.

You can earn money from a variety of different sources online and those sources are expanding every single day. This is why I have stressed learning and taking courses so much throughout. The more information and skills you have, the more tasks and projects you can undertake. Even if you know the very basics of, let's say, logo design, then you can easily learn the more advanced practices as you complete projects.

Some people would probably advise you to pick one skill and stick to it. I, however, would advise you to put multiple eggs across every basket you can find. Not only will this increase your sources of revenue, but it will also give you the experience in many different areas which can come in useful later down the line.

Also, if one revenue stream doesn't take off or fails, you have another to fall back on. I have used this method for many years and have found that it has helped me in figuring out what I actually enjoy doing; the benefits are endless, don't let anyone else tell you otherwise.

More importantly, I will give you some ideas of revenue streams below that you can seek out, but be aware that not all of them will be successful. These ideas are not there for you to make thousands, but merely to provide you with dribs and drabs of money as extra revenue. If you are looking to make a revenue stream heavily profitable for yourself, then ideally, you should be investing a large amount of your time and effort into it.

Revenue Stream Ideas

Stock investing

Instagram flipping

Writing on Medium

One-off projects on UpWork

Selling photos & videos on stock sites

Running a niche blog

Starting a podcast

Writing a book

Consulting

DON'T FORGET ABOUT TRAVEL

Throughout most of this e-book, I have discussed money, working, and problems but haven't really touched on one of the most important aspects - travel. I would consider myself an expert in travel as I have lived in multiple different countries and continents for over 6 years of my life and have travelled to other countries for 10 years. I have travelled both as a digital nomad and as a full-time traveller.

I am going to assume that the primary reason you are reading this book is that you want to travel whilst being able to sustain yourself. Of course, there are options that allow some people to travel with unlimited money (parents etc.) and there are also options where you can work physically when you travel. Ignoring the unlimited money option, I don't believe personally that you can enjoy the same flexibility and freedom with physical jobs than you do with remote work.

When it comes to physical job you actually have a time schedule, a boss, and the chances are you won't be paid very well. Jobs for travellers are very limited and do not usually involve high-paying jobs. Perhaps this isn't an issue for you as you are only looking for income to sustain your travel plans. However, did you stop to consider the prices of meals out, tours, attractions, and other experiences you want while you are travelling?

This is where many people slip up. They believe that earning enough to move from hostel to hostel, eating a meal, and relaxing on the beach is travelling. It can be if that's the way you want to travel but there will always be something that comes up that you really want to do and it is essential you have the funds to cover that.

Let's say that you earn $1,000 US per month from a physical job while travelling and then break the expenses down:

Accommodation - $600 Per Month

Food - $100 Per Month (Very Basic)

Transport - $50 Per Month

Now that is just the very basic expenses. Let's take a look at all the other expenses that could occur with your $250 left:

New Flight - $200-$1000

Bungee Jump - $100 - 300

Skydive - $100 - 300

Tours - $100 - $1000

Night Out - $20 - $100

Renting a Car - $80 - $500

Internet - $20 - $60

Meal Out - $20 - $120

Now that is just to give you an idea of the things you might do when you travel. If you visit a country for 1 month only, get a physical job, and want to do every tour, you will not be able to afford it. Also, you will probably not get the time to do them due to your working hours.

The reason for mentioning this is to compare it to remote work and why being a digital nomad is the more preferable option.

Take the finances for instance, you have no cap on what you can earn. You could do a project that takes you a week and earn $1000 USD from it, which is the same as your monthly salary in my example. Obviously, it depends on your skillset, experience, and luck, but add that together with multiple other revenue streams and your possibilities are endless.

This is why I recommend having 1 main source of income and multiple small sources; you can use the main income to supplement your basic necessities and use the small sources for all the extra things you want to do.

Not only will you be more in control of your finances, but you will also have the free time available. Say you wanted to do a tour that only ran every Monday 9 am to 1 pm, with a physical job, you may be scheduled to work every weekday from 9-5 but when you are your own boss, you can do the tour, and start work at 2 pm for instance.

It might seem contradictory for me to stress about putting hard work and dedication into remote work and then talk about travelling and enjoying yourself, but at the end of the day, that is what a digital nomad does.

Think about it this way, you may only have this digital nomad lifestyle available for 2 years, you are getting the chance to travel the world and do things some could only dream of, don't waste it by focusing all your efforts on work. I have learned that lesson from my own mistakes and I think it is essential to share with you.

One important note that I will mention, is that you should never declare that you work online when you enter an airport and go through security. I have witnessed situations where others have stated that they earned income online, they were then whisked off for interviews and potentially refused entry to the country.

This is because the Governments do not want people earning money where they cannot track it and where travellers could try and live in that country for more time than allowed. I am not telling you to lie, but you should exaggerate the truth so it doesn't come back to bite you.

To make it clear, you should take the time to enjoy seeing every new part of the world you travel to. You don't know how long it's going to be there. I have had the luxury of visiting some beautiful places in the world before they were damaged or destroyed by earthquakes, fires, volcanic eruptions, and even war.

Without trying to sound cheesy, life really does fly by when you travelling, make sure you take every moment in and forget about any pointless worries you may have. The best advice I can give when travelling is to never say NO.

> *"take the time to enjoy seeing every new part of the world you travel to. You don't know how long it's going to be there."*

IS THIS FOR YOU?

In this guide, I've talked thoroughly on the digital nomad lifestyle in the hope of accurately educating you, giving you a clearer picture of what you should expect and hopefully making you question whether or not this is the right move for you.

I felt this was particularly important as many articles online regarding the digital nomad lifestyle often sell young people on the lifestyle with the false representation of 'you get to sit on a beach and type when you feel like it'. It's never quite that simple, and though there may be days you get to do that (if you're lucky), that is in no way an accurate representation of the day to day digital nomad lifestyle.

I find it hard to comprehend why these websites attempt to sell you on the lifestyle in this way, having clearly not researched it properly before they make those claims.

That's where the idea for this guide stemmed from. Giving you a fair but overall positive representation of the digital nomad lifestyle whilst informing you of the obstacles that may stand in your way if you choose the path. I want you to have the best success possible in whatever you choose to do, whether it's as a digital nomad or going back to a conventional nine to five.

I've said throughout this guide that the life of a digital nomad requires serious thought and definitely isn't suited to everybody, you need to find a career that best suits who you are. But if you're strong-willed, thick-skinned and ready for a new challenge then this may just be the way forward for you.

It's important to take the information that you've learned in this guide, compile what you've learned and then use the information to decide "Is this for me?". Ask yourself, then ask yourself again. Weigh up your options and really look within for the answer. If you're ready for a new challenge and still think this might be it, then it's certainly worth a shot - providing you're willing to make the necessary changes to your life.

Good luck in your journey as a digital nomad, if that's what you choose to do. Ahead is an entire world of opportunities with many new experiences to be taken advantage of, you just need to have the fighting spirit to survive and thrive.

> *"A successful digital nomad; the ability to survive and thrive outside the norm".*

End

THANK YOU

Note From the Author: Reviews are gold to authors! If you've enjoyed this book, would you consider rating it and reviewing on Amazon!

If you would like any advice regarding any topic within this book, please do not hesitate to reach out to me on the email below:

chadrwyatt@gmail.com

As mentioned previously, I wanted to provide you with a list of sites where you can search for remote jobs and freelance websites:

UpWork
Fiverr
PeoplePerHour
WeWorkRemotely
Jobspresso
Remote.co
Indeed (Search for remote)
Hubstaff
BeaFreelanceBlogger (Writing Jobs)
VIPKid (Teaching)
Qkids (Teaching)
FlexJobs
Angellist
Shopify (E-commerce)
Etsy (Selling items you make)
Working Nomads

All rights reserved. No portion of this book may be reproduced in any form without permission from the author, except as permitted by copyright law. For permissions contact:

chadrwyatt@gmail.com

Cover by Chad Wyatt.

© 2020 Chad Wyatt

Made in the USA
Columbia, SC
23 January 2025